Cruel Tricks of the Heart

~Jonez

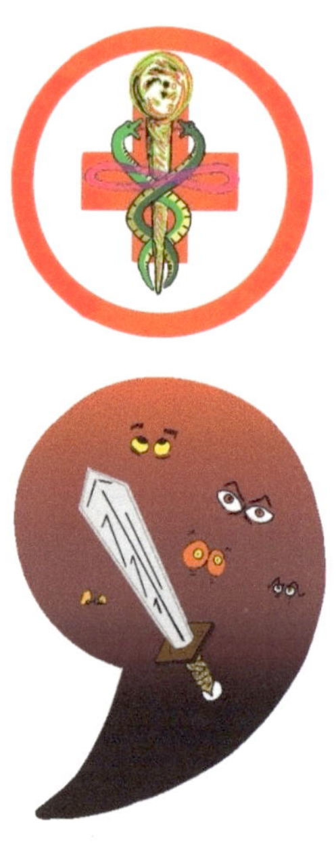

I WANT TO DEDICATE THIS BOOK TO MY CHILDREN ETHAN AND KAYA. BECAUSE OF THE TWO OF YOU I LIVE, AND FOR THE TWO OF YOU I'D GIVE MY LIFE. -DADDY LOVES YOU.

Prologue

In an attempt to share the thoughts and feelings of one with mental illness, my first book was written. Tormented was a short rendition of what was to be a two volume book. But as I began working on this I felt compelled to make it a little less artsy. So I I'd and with it a new title and focus. Same goal.

So here we have a depiction of the five most prevalent issues we deal with today and how they all intertwine sooner are later. Also thru an understanding of them I've tried to share some advice. To help you cope or help you help your loved ones. I am not a licensed physician and in no way should be held responsible for anyone's health whom doesn't take my advice . Please share with everyone.

TABLE OF CONTENTS

YOU EVER IMAGINE ?

CHAPTER 1

DEPRESSION

"Depression is being colorblind and constantly told how colorful the world is "~Atticus

Where do I start? Everyone gets down at times. But imagine one day you wake up to find you've lost the feeling, the emotion of happy. And there ain't no shaking back. Day in and day out you wait for it to return. Till you start to notice your whole life coming to a stop, because without happiness you lose your drive, your ability to care. You lose all that makes you a functioning,social,individual.

Then slowly you notice yourself beginning to sleep more and more. Communication with others is becoming almost nonexistent. You stop eating and your hygiene becomes of little concern. You literally begin to go for days without eating or bathing.

Soon the more separated you get from the world , the more vigorously you

attempt to sleep forever. Like you want to live in your dreams , but that's only a short fix. Soon when that fails to please you is when death starts to look appealing.

And understand what I'm about to tell you. If you were an addict or became one looking to find the joy you lost, that shit will even begin to lose your interest sooner or later. I say that because in a depression someone will always come along and try to make you think it's the drugs that have you that way. Like a guilt trip to excuse themselves from trying to put any actual effort into helping you. Well, tell me this then, what's it mean when I've been lost the want to even get high at all? What's keeping me depressed then? As I become comfortable in my miserable sorrow.

When I don't even want to be happy again and I find peace in the feeling of not having feelings. When the death of you is my focus because I can only get satisfaction from killing myself just once. But I can kill you and you and you and enjoy this blissful feeling like an everlasting fix. Because my fix begins to come from being a sadist. Yes your pain becomes my pleasure. Insane ain't it? Well, it's only the beginning. It's not as simple as it seems from the outside lookin in.

See depression is a complex illness, despite how cut and dry it seems to an onlooker. It takes a long time for even the person suffering to understand what's going on inside them. You can't explain what you yourself don't understand. There lies one problem with getting help. If you think it's just a bad day or two and it'll get better. Surely you can't fathom having this go on indefinitely, it's just not how it works. This is how most consult themselves.

Usually by the time one understands that what their going through isn't just a bad day, they've already lost the care we talked about earlier. Leaving them to marinate in their own sadness. And usually no one really inquires in-depth, so it can go on unnoticed.

Then if your lucky you have a good day. This should be the opportunity you take to find help. But no, you feel there's no need because it's over. And how would

The madness got to you too?
Sure Did...
Mind
Body
Mommy?
Maddness is the last stop when slipping thru Insanity & once you arrive you find it's a one way trip, no returns. And the Show begins.
The Soul

you explain this anyway especially if it's not happening anymore. You might seem like your just complaining about life. Stop! This cycle is the death of some. It repeats and repeats till they convince themselves no one cares and life isn't worth living any longer. Because they never reached out and made it known they were suffering and no one ever inquired. The whole thing went unnoticed till ,well.... There's no reset in life, don't go unnoticed.

We'll all face depression in our lives at one time or another. It's natural, but don't mistake clinical depression for just a bad day. It's a serious matter. You think it won't happen to you because your to strong minded, I did too. We have no control over some of life's curve balls. You never know when the unexpected will happen and completely change your world. I didn't.

Never think that a child is too young to have these problems. All my life I was told I was too young to be depressed. Then at 24 when I made the choice to get help, I had already been suffering for years. Now add on some real life traumatic experiences, I was living in a deep dark corner of my soul. I hadn't truly knew how it felt to be happy for years. And I had been ready to die for just as long.

The right help is priceless. I had to learn the hard way. I initially went to my regular physician. That resulted in me leaving with a bag full of prescriptions. I was on everything. And it didn't take long to find out that wasn't my best decision, when I started having horrible side effects.   Plus the medicine wasn't really   working, only keeping me so out of it I couldn't explain what I was feeling to anyone. So I took the advice doctors always give about researching your ailment yourself. Truth is no one can understand how you feel and what will change that better than you.

So I discovered a medication that seemed to be exactly what I needed. This time I went to an actual mental health doctor and I explained my situation. After showing them the medicine I wanted to try they prescribed it. What an amazing feeling to be happy again.

And with only one miracle pill, so I thought.

Because it was a new drug and I was so anxious to get better, I didn't research as much as I should have. Turns out I'm forever at the mercy of this drug. I can never get off it because without it I'm worse off than I was originally. And it'll never stop getting worse.

I didn't say that to say don't take the medication. No. I said that to emphasize the dangers of one not knowing enough about what you put in your body. And two don't depend solely on the pills. You also have to be proactive in natural ways that increase your serotonin output in conjunction with the medicine. I'm not saying you'll ever be completely healed because it's not something that just goes away. But you can live a much better quality of life than depression was going to allow otherwise.

In conclusion don't give up. Good days will come and go. Eventually you'll learn to understand your triggers and such and avoid letting yourself be a victim to yourself. As my friend Mr. Richard Jones stated" all days can't be the best, but what you doin with the rest? "Hope.

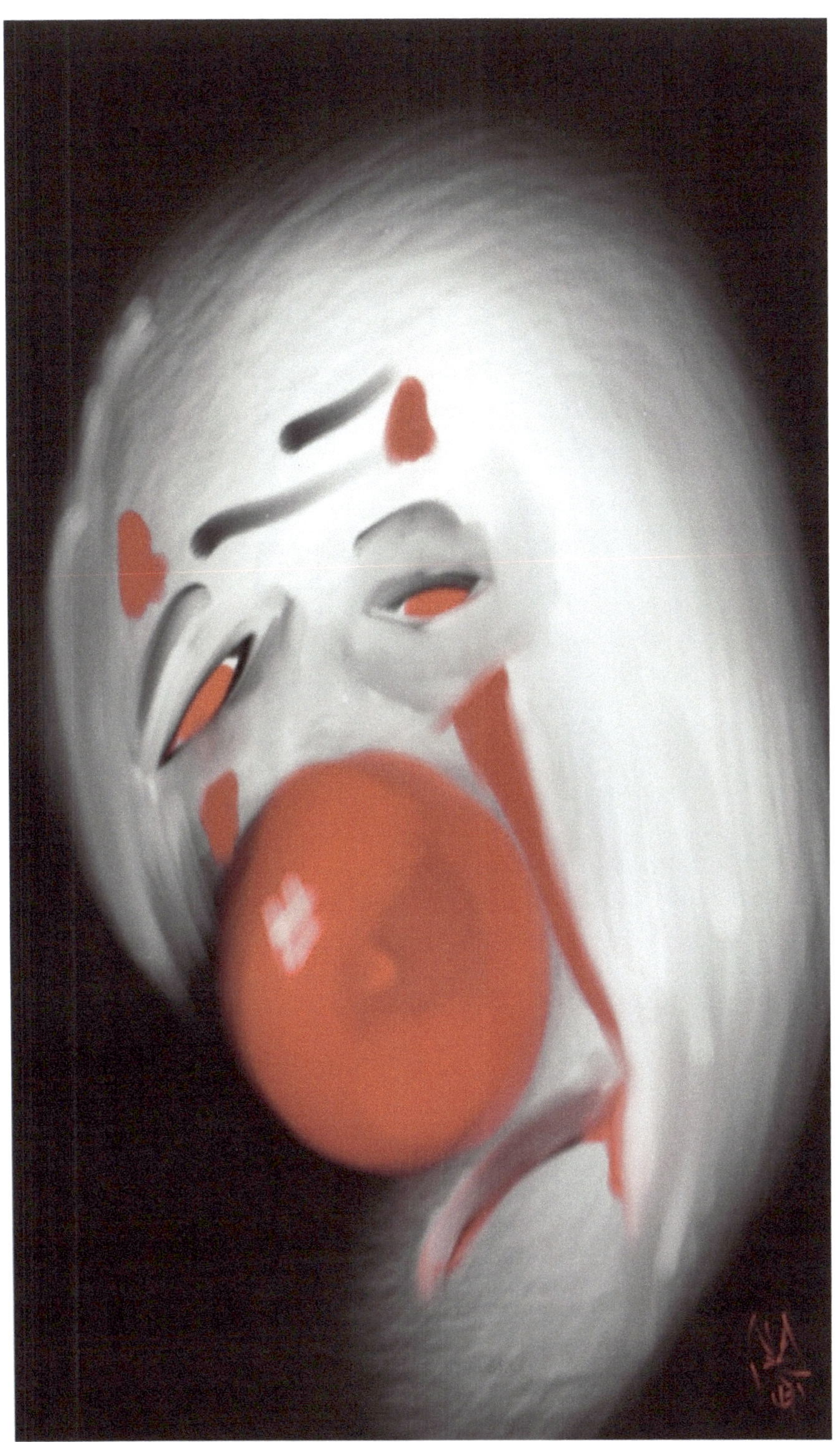

"Therefore do not be anxious about tomorrow, for tomorrow will be anxious for itself. Sufficient for the day is its own trouble.

Chapter 2

ANXIETY

"This is what an OG told me, filthy rich and dying lonely. Fuck a Benz and fuck a Rollie , life is what you make it homie"~Carlos Coy

You ever feel just a little bit worried about the bills or a new job? Of course it's normal, it's also nothing close to what severe anxiety feels like. And if you've never experienced it, it almost seems as if the person is over reacting. I used to feel the same way about people that said they had anxiety attacks, till I experienced my first one.

Imagine waking up and feeling as if you were in the middle of a deadly gun battle or riding in a car going the wrong way on the interstate. That feeling of impending doom. Now image you know none of this is really happening, your safe in your home but the feeling persists. How do you explain to

someone you feel like you could die at any minute when they can see your perfectly safe?

It can start small and build into tremors. Then hyperventilating and aspirating. Your muscles seize and you begin to blackout. All because you woke up in a rush or maybe had a lot to get done today. There's no warning and almost never an actual reason for it. There's not a whole lot one can say about anxiety, it's like talking about Hiroshima, it happened, let's hope it doesn't happen again.

My family has a history of people suffering from anxiety. I remember when I was young my grandmother got so bad she couldn't go anywhere. A simple trip to the grocery store became a nightmare for her. Eventually closing her self away from the world. Today she has to keep her headphones with her everywhere she goes. By listening to the music she's able to focus on something other than her anxiety. Myself I keep busy with my phone or tablet. People usually think I'm ignoring them but I'm just trying to focus.

Just know no matter how much anxiety feels like the death of you, it's not. It can be controlled. It's not easy at first but with time you can understand what sets you off and find a distraction. Find your headphones or phone that'll work for you. I've even heard a guy say he just closes his eyes and thinks of the color pink. Anything that calms you is worth meditating on.

Peaceful surroundings and a routine to keep from having too many unexpected changes in your day will help. One day at a time, live for today, tomorrow has its own worries.

Adict
Your
Never
Alone
He's
Always
there
With
you
Just
open
your
eyes
close
your
tears
and will
be
right
there
100%

CHAPTER 3

ADDICTION

"Don't spend a lifetime trying to get rid of old habits, just spend a day trying to make one worth having."~Crucifix

Addiction, this is a complicated subject seeing how it comes in so many forms. On so many levels, for so many reasons. You can be addicted to anything from food to sex, even things like television or love. It's caused for so many reasons. Some for comfort, some from indulgence. But all end in over indulging.

Sometimes in life things happen that can cause a person to feel insecure or even unhappy. When this occurs we almost always find something to feel that void. This becomes a habit and without limits it can become an addiction. A habit is something we do subconsciously from time to time, while addiction is something we consciously pursue for pleasure. We can

become either mentally or physically dependent on our addiction depending on the substance.

But let's talk about drugs. While some believe because a doctor has prescribed their medications they aren't at risk or can't be considered an addict. False. History shows time and again how the government has made substances illegal to turn around and put half the country on a legal synthetic form of the same chemical. Which we know now from several mishaps that these synthetic drugs are way worse and more deadly than the original substance. So when you feel like I can't do today without my Xanax or my son is out of control he has to have his Ritalin. You have an addiction, which was once cured by simple marijuana or your son is now hooked on the governments personal crystal meth recipe. Yea it's facts.

So when it comes to addiction I choose to separate people in two distinct categories. One an addict, a person who does drugs to feel high to feel good. They tend to consume as much of every substance available, not stopping till it's all gone. In an attempt to kill some pain they have hidden inside. They say, their just buzzed when they can barely say the words without slurring and/or *drooling on themselves and passing out. Or they have been up for days with out eating or sleeping and think that everything is normal. When it's obvious their body is shutting down.*

They will continue to do this till either they choose to stop or they die. There's no in between. They can't have just one. They will always indulge. And you will see them change moods dramatically in the presence of drugs.

Then there is what we call a functioning addict. Someone that understands their body chemistry enough to know what is lacking. So without a doctor and the synthetic government drugs, they are able to use what they need when they need it as much as is needed. You will notice these people take drugs daily and you almost never see them show signs of being loaded. They function normally and productively hence the term functioning addict.

Some people are high strung or always nervous and need help balancing out. Others have a lack of energy or concentration and need to be stimulated. And can achieve these things without the help of a professional. There's also people like I said in the beginning that believe only a doctor knows how to fix them and if it wasn't prescribed by one it's no good. It will have you addicted and since it's illegal it has to be bad. Disregard their nonsense completely. Those people still think marijuana kills and alcohol is perfectly fine and harmless.

Choosing to use drugs for reasons like depression and anxiety can be dangerous. For an addict that doesn't know how to stop it can drive them further into their suffering. They will tend to use the wrong substance at the wrong time. For instance they might take a bunch of downers to feel good when depressed. That will only accelerate the process of depression making it harder to come out of. Or they could take stimulants for anxiety thinking since stimulants make them more social they shouldn't be nervous. No, it will only cause you to have uncontrollable anxiety which could result in numerous complications most of which could be life threatening.

I hear people often attribute the cause of people's mental illness to drugs. But in reality that's completely false. There are just as many people mentally ill that have never done drugs. And people that aren't addicts. Will tell you even the drugs lose there magic when your severely Ill. It's like getting high becomes a waste of time when you can't feel or feel too much. And you jus want it all to end.

I've been around drugs my entire life. My earliest memories of my father were seeing him sit on the other side the bed with his back to me. All I could see and hear were smoke and bubbling water. There was this distinct aroma about it. My dad drank regularly, he'd even share with my grandpas dogs if they were around. Over the years I learned of his experiences with all types of drugs.

Personally I was 12 or 13 the first time I was offered marijuana. And I remember the very next day inquiring about how to get more. An inquiry that began a life long journey. But that's a story for another time. By 14 I had experimented with every pill the doctor gave my grandmother to help her depression and anxiety. Which we now know as the cocktail loritab, Xanax, and somas. Cocaine by the time I was 15. LSD at 18 and an extended stay in ecstasy by the time I was 19. And on and on. By the time I was 25 I almost can't remember getting loaded except I know I got high continuously. Because by that point I learned what my body needed and what it didn't.

People ask what am I using and I tell them it changes with the seasons. Because my mental illness never stays the same forever. I can suffer severe depression for a time. I can change and deal with anxiety for a time. So I medicate according. Don't get me wrong sometimes I get the urge to get wasted and have fun, but I usually don't because I know what over indulging can do to my mental health. And I've struggled too long to be counter productive.

Before I end this I want to touch on the other things I mentioned. Like food addiction, it may not be illegal or even instant death but it can be life threatening. Overeating in itself is very unhealthy. Sex, this addiction causes people to act in ways that can be very dangerous for numerous reasons. What I'm saying is in life over indulging is never a good thing. You need to learn your own boundaries. You can never create boundaries based on someone else. Your chemistry is not the same. What's healthy for you isn't gonna be healthy for everyone else. And learn to educate your children about learning their bodies also. Don't let them grow up depending on the opinion of someone who's only job is to have you prescribed to what ever drug the company sponsoring them is pushing that

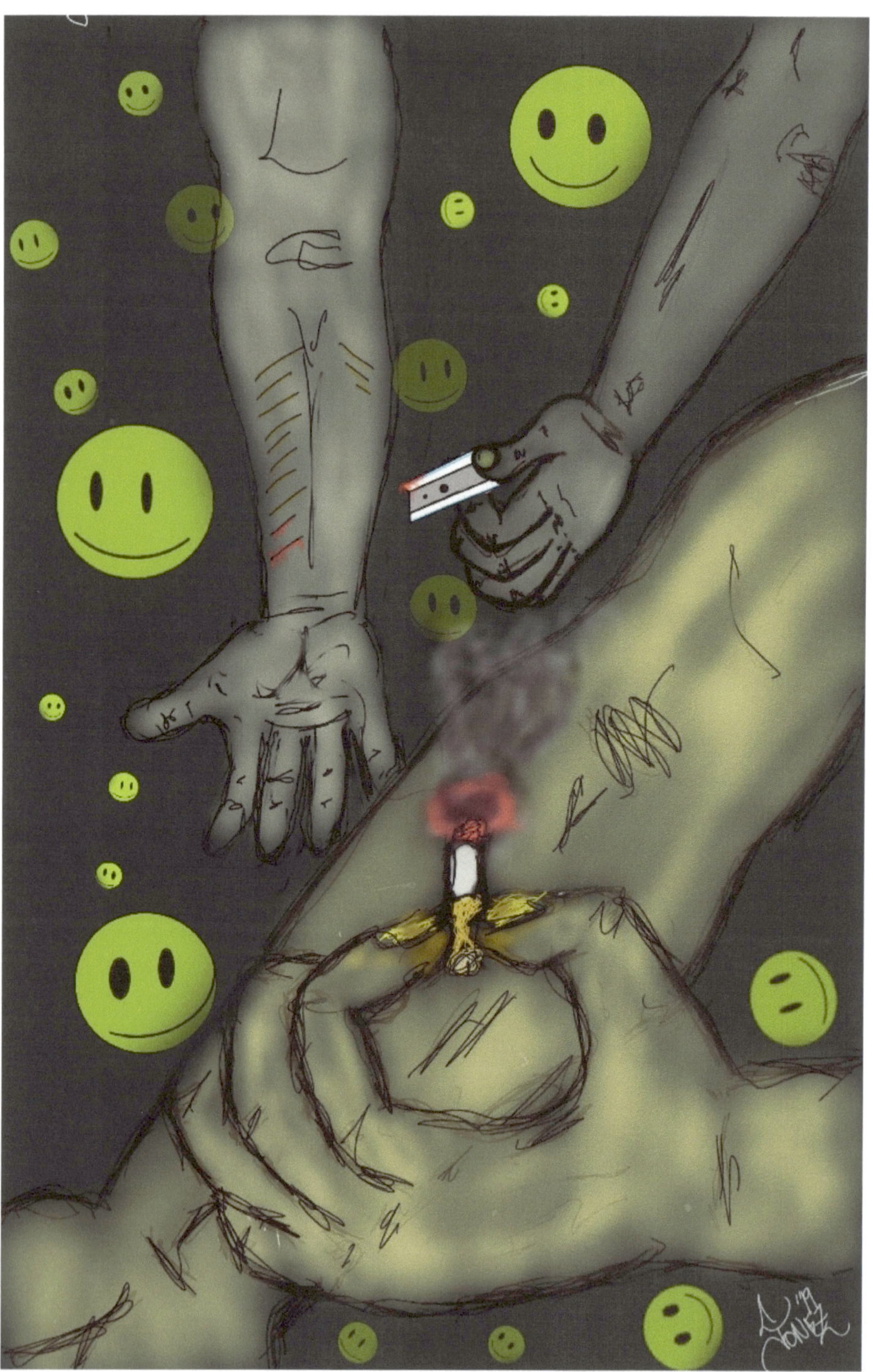

Chapter 4

SELF-HARM

"I hurt myself today, to see if I still feel"
~Trent Reznor

Where do you begin to talk about a subject so taboo such as this one. It's very rare to hear about self-harm, no one talks about abusing themselves as much as you'd think they would. I mean it's natural to speak up when someone is hurting you. So why is it hurting ourselves is such a secretive act. Is it because it's basically one step from killing ourself. Almost like conditioning ours_. This is when they will take something sharp usually a razor and make small cuts on there body.   Usually in very discrete locations. And often they will apply alcohol to the wounds to get multiple satisfactions from each cut.

Why you ask? See when you experience pain without shock, which is a more prominent feeling. What you get is the pleasure of feeling your brain releasing a wave of endorphins. If you don't know that's a good feeling. Basically your brain trying to help with your pain naturally. And since it's a chemical in your brain it also can relieve other forms of pain that normally have no cure. Like the pain of a broken heart. This is why it's so addictive.

And in some ways it becomes routine also. People often get hooked on the feeling they get. And like drugs can abuse it. Before they know they're cutting for every reason they can find. Till it's not giving the same pleasure so they're doing it more and more chasing a high.

There's other ways of achieving this like burning. Whipping yourself, no not a spanking. Fully chastising yourself. You can even achieve this thru adrenaline from near death experiences. Like drowning or suffocating yourself.

No matter your method it's all the same and it's all dangerous, unhealthy, and potentially deadly. You can't get that feeling. So you continue to cut till you've went too far. Now all you can do is bleed out. With no hope of being able to reverse what you've done, your only option is to watch your life end as your blood pools around you.

Sad but truly the fate of too many people. I'm not sure if it can be categorized here but I'm gonna do it. Having a self destructive nature. You may not be intending to physically hurt yourself but even if you can avoid it the mental pain you cause yourself is plenty.

You know someone we all do that constantly makes decisions that they know will end badly for them? Regardless they choose to let it happen over and over. Their self destructive which is no different than self harm. Only they are trying to cause their pain through no fault of their own.

I've burnt for some time. I honestly remember the first time vividly. It was my 24th birthday. I was alone getting myself high as usual. This was at the peak of my depression not long before I chose to seek help. I used the half inch thick blunt I was smoking and began to create a smiley face on top my left hand. In the fatty area by the thumb. I remember watching it heal I focused a lot on my burn. And I liked to touch it. Because in the beginning it still hurt. And that comforted me inside.

I never forgot that birthday or that pain and eventually when nothing else was left I went back to it. It feels so good and Unlike most I'm not ashamed of my scars. I tell *anyone who asks what they are. Why? This way there's no confusion as to the seriousness of my mental illness. This is not play time. And I am not playing pretend.*

If you choose to hurt yourself don't keep it to yourself. It could be the only way for someone to take your illness serious. It wasn't till one day on the phone with my wife. After we had been going through some things that she insinuated to me she was a cutter. She said I'd never have known if I wasn't told because she had become so good at hiding the cuts. Same with her sadness. She was so good at putting on that smile I never would have known she was suffering so had she not told me this. It hurt me because I knew she was in pain to do this and also she exposed it so I would understand her pain.

If you are hurting enough to harm yourself you shouldn't keep it to yourself. Tell someone , reach out. Get help before is not enough and you do something that you can't take back. Your life is important. And it's important to others even if you can't see it, it is.

CHAPTER 5

SUICIDE

" DO THEY REALLY CHOOSE THEIR OWN TIME TO GO ? OR WAS IT PART OF HIS PLAN ALL ALONG ? ~JONEZ

Wow, this will possibly be the most difficult words I've ever had to write. Everything in this book has been at sometime in my life a reality. But this is a reality I never wish upon anyone. The questions your left with. The demons you battle. The empty place where someone should be. It's like they left too early and life don't know how to adjusted. Gods plan is out of balance.

Why is always the first question for us. But on the other hand, for the people with all these demons we have talked about. The better question is why not? Either way we're left wondering what could cause someone to finally give up. To feel they will never be able to correct whatever it is that's

wrong. To think there families wouldn't be devastated and torn apart. Some say it's selfish. Others say it's coward. Some even call it the easy way out.   Call it what you will but it's still a travesty.

In order to do this let's step in their shoes and really get a play by play of what all leads up to this and the actual preparation. That way we can understand the difficult decisions that have to be made for this to happen.

So I'm going to give it to you from my view but no one knows for sure seeing how we can't ask someone experienced. Let's say our subject has been suffering from some anxiety. And try's to stimulate their self to shake back. But this leads to seclusion and eventually depression. The more depressed they become the less social and productive they become. These things lead to feelings of worthlessness and being unwanted.

Once someone starts to feel there life has no value a few downers help numb the pain and make it easier to harm their self. Sometimes it's deliberate like cutting or burning. But then sometimes it's done and not realized that it's even happening. Someone could literally be harming themselves repeatedly and not understand it's deliberate. Then in order to accept that have begun to enjoy the pain, they have to except that they have become a masochist. That's just too shameful to face.

So now the drugs have little to no affect and hurting themselves has lost its edge. The feeling of despair and self hate set in. Now it all starts to become an actual thought. How would I do it? How will my family feel? What will my kids think? I'm sure they can go on without me. It'll be easier for them than to live with me this way. Or even, they'll get what they wanted. I'll make them hurt the way I do.

With all this going through your head it can be easy to forget the truth of it all. That your stronger than this and this short time won't last forever. But you have to endure to find out.

At this point had they not found reason to live, they consider their options. Most people have certain fears of dying and this will usually affect their choice of method. Now that their ready it's time. The thought of harming themselves is gone after all the self harm preparation. The second thoughts have been put to rest. The last obstacle is mainly are you man enough to say you made a mistake and face your loved ones? Or do you have to continue because you've already crossed that line?

Never be ashamed to say you were wrong. Especially if it means the difference between life and death. Your life affects more people in more ways than you'll ever understand in a lifetime. It'll never fix things or make someone else's life easier to take your life. It will all ways be devastating. And if you have children, do you want them to have to live with the thought you were a coward or you didn't love them enough to stay?

In my life suicide has crossed my path more times than I would have liked. From my cousins mom. To kids in school giving up. Getting a call my sons godfather shot himself. I've even had two friends in the same week kill themselves. At 9 years old I had to listen to my mom tell me about her attempts. And on and on the list is endless.

Then there's my plight. Over the years I've wanted to die plenty. I chose overdose. But God didn't feel it was my time. After tryin countless times and being miraculously saved when I shouldn't have. I mean I was alone and God shook me back at the last minute every time. I started to think I wouldn't be allowed to leave early. There must be a reason. Then the last time I tried. I was alone locked in a small bathroom. I had consumed almost seven grams of meth in under 45 minutes. My heart was giving out. I could feel it slowly stopping like it didn't have the strength to pump anymore. It had sprinted a mile and was threw.

As it slowed and I felt it take its last beat. I began to fall forward off the toilet I was sitting on as everything became a blur. Then just as the lights went out, I felt a hand from behind me. It gripped my shoulder as if it were catching me from falling and saying I'm here. In that moment the thought of someone grabbing me when I'm alone locked in this small bathroom was startling. The shock jolted my heart which began to beat normally again.

It was a miracle. God chose to give me this gift. He chose to show me how much he loved me by taking the time to personally save me.   And for that I promised to never try and kill myself again. I'll die in the time and manner he has written for me.

Always remember anything can be forgiven and all transgressions from yesterday have been forgotten in the

heart of God. Today might be cloudy but tomorrow is brand new.

Timothy Ryder you'll always be my friend and brother
R.I.P BRUH we'll meet again on the other side.

CONCLUSION

In conclusion life's not a perfect situation that'll never go horribly wrong. So be prepared for what ever may come about. And remember it's not the end of the world there's always tomorrow. Last but definitely most important, suicide isn't an answer. It's only excuse to not try. Not try to understand, not try to get help, not try to endure and persevere. You better than that. God made you to overcome, so fight the devil. And triumph.

ABOUT THE AUTHOR

Like I said I've dealt with all these things at some point in my life. And still do. I wanted to attempt to bring it to the public from the point of view of a victim. Not that their wrong but textbooks and lectures can only prepare a doctor so much. But it will never teach them the full complexity of mental illness. We don't understand the full complexity. It's ever changing day to day. Emotions are unique fragile things. And we've yet master them. Also I wrote this to shed light on suicide I've lost too many friends. The world has lost too many lives. Help stop this from happening to someone you love.

Thank you God for guiding me through this and and being with me till the end. All glory and all credit is yours alone Amen. I love you ABBA.

THE NUGLIFE COLLECTIVE ETC...
@STUDIO FO'20
Copyright © August 15,2019
S.P.L.